OXFORD
UNIVERSITY PRESS

Great Clarendon Street, Oxford, OX2 6DP, United Kingdom

Oxford University Press is a department of the University of Oxford. It furthers the University's objective of excellence in research, scholarship, and education by publishing worldwide. Oxford is a registered trade mark of Oxford University Press in the UK and in certain other countries

Text © Oxford University Press 2024

Illustrations © Lala Stellune 2024

The moral rights of the author have been asserted

First Edition published in 2024

All rights reserved. No part of this publication may be reproduced, stored in a retrieval system, or transmitted, in any form or by any means, without the prior permission in writing of Oxford University Press, or as expressly permitted by law, by licence or under terms agreed with the appropriate reprographics rights organization. Enquiries concerning reproduction outside the scope of the above should be sent to the Rights Department, Oxford University Press, at the address above.

You must not circulate this work in any other form and you must impose this same condition on any acquirer

British Library Cataloguing in Publication Data

Data available

ISBN: 978-1-382-04373-1

10 9 8 7 6 5 4 3 2 1

The manufacturing process conforms to the environmental regulations of the country of origin.

Printed in China by Golden Cup.

Acknowledgements

Blackbeard: Fact or Fiction? written by Ben Hubbard

Content on pages 7, 64, 66 and 70 written by Suzy Ditchburn

Illustrated by Lala Stellune

Author photo courtesy of Ben Hubbard

The publisher and author would like to thank the following for permission to use photographs and other copyright material:

Photos: Cover: Andrey_Kuzmin/Shutterstock; p2, p12: Everett Collection/Shutterstock; p13: Pictorial Press Ltd/Alamy Stock Photo; p15: Lebrecht Music & Arts/Alamy Stock Photo; p20, p62 (tl): Stocksnapper/Shutterstock; p34, p63 (br): Fer Gregory/Shutterstock; p35, p63 (bl): Chronicle/Alamy Stock Photo; p42: Associated Press/Alamy Stock Photo; p43 (t): Tatohra/Shutterstock; p43 (m), p63 (m): Paolo Gallo/Shutterstock; p43 (b): Millenius/Shutterstock; p47: Keith Corrigan/Alamy Stock Photo; p51, p62 (bl): mauritius images GmbH/Alamy Stock Photo; p52, p63 (t): Penta Springs Limited/Alamy Stock Photo; p56: GL Archive/Alamy Stock Photo; p57: Scisetti Alfio/Shutterstock; p58, p62 (r): Iconographic Archive/Alamy Stock Photo; p59: PictureLux/The Hollywood Archive/Alamy Stock Photo.

Every effort has been made to contact copyright holders of material reproduced in this book. Any omissions will be rectified in subsequent printings if notice is given to the publisher.

BLACKBEARD: FACT OR FICTION?

Written by Ben Hubbard
Illustrated by Lala Stellune

OXFORD
UNIVERSITY PRESS

READ THIS BOOK IF...

YOU LOVE

AMAZING FACTS

AND LEARNING ABOUT

HISTORY!

STOP AND THINK

In this book you will find out all about Blackbeard, a famous pirate.

You'll learn the myths people believed about Blackbeard, as well as facts about his life.

What is the difference between a myth and a fact?

CONTENTS

Pirate sighting 10

Edward Teach 20

Pirate trainee 24

Captain Teach 32

Blackbeard: the legend 46

Blackbeard's end 52

Glossary 60

Index 62

PIRATE SIGHTING

In 1717, sailors were **shocked**. Ships sailing along North America's east coast were being attacked by pirates.

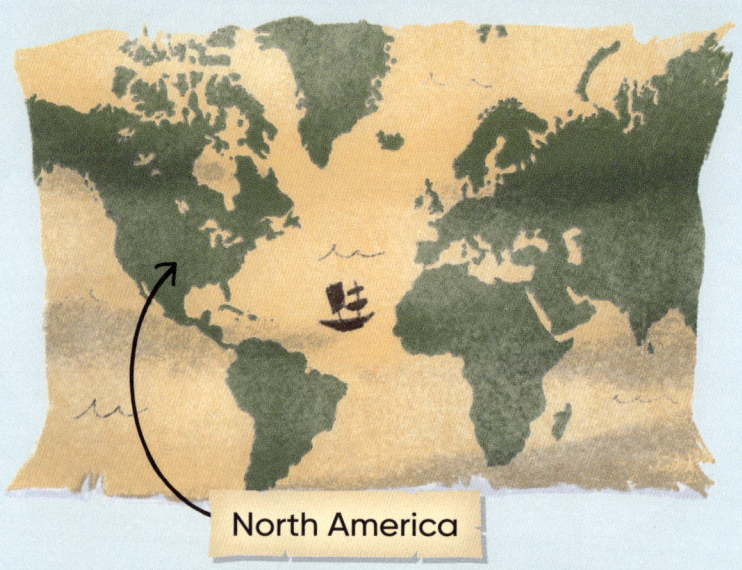

North America

Some ships were set on fire and sunk. Other ships had their **cargo** stolen, but their **crews** were set free.

Sailors spoke of a pirate ship with a black flag. The ship appeared suddenly. It *sped* towards them, with cannons firing.

Scarier still was a tall pirate who was the ship's captain. He looked more like a **MONSTER** than a man. His name? Blackbeard!

Fact or fake?

Were pirates heroes?

A pirate is someone who attacks ships and steals their cargo. In films and books, pirates are sometimes shown as **heroes**. However, most were dangerous criminals.

Bad things often happened to them:

Captain Kidd (1645–1701)
Fate: **hanged** for piracy

Mary Read (1685–1721)
Fate: arrested and died in jail

John Julian (1701–1733)
Fate: sold as an **enslaved** person

Anne Bonny (1697–1721)
Fate: disappeared

Blackbeard terrified everyone who saw him.

This is how he looked:

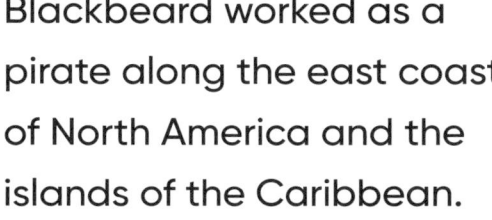

Blackbeard worked as a pirate along the east coast of North America and the islands of the Caribbean.

Feared and famous

Soon, everyone had heard of Blackbeard. He became the world's most **famous** and feared pirate.

People said that Blackbeard was **bloodthirsty** and cruel. They said he attacked ships, and killed the crews.

Blackbeard attacks a ship.

Blackbeard caused fear and panic wherever he went. Ships would scatter rather than fight him.

However, were the stories about Blackbeard **true?** Read on to learn the truth about Blackbeard.

EDWARD TEACH

We don't know much about Blackbeard's childhood. His name was probably Edward Teach. Experts think he was born in Bristol, England, in 1680.

Bristol

Many ships sailed from Bristol to North America and the Caribbean. These areas were controlled by Britain, Spain and France at that time.

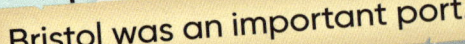
Bristol was an important port.

Teach worked for the **British Navy** during Queen Anne's War. He fought against Spain and France.

During the war, some **privately-owned** ships fought for Britain. These ships attacked enemy **merchant ships**. The private crews could then keep the cargo from the merchant ships. The people on these private ships were called privateers.

When Queen Anne's War ended, privateers were **no longer allowed** to attack ships. However, some continued anyway.

privateer

These privateers became **PIRATES**.

pirate

Edward Teach became a pirate, too.

Edward Teach

PIRATE TRAINEE

In 1716, Teach joined the crew of pirate captain **Benjamin Hornigold**.

Teach was a *fast learner*. Before long, Hornigold put him in command of his own ship.

When pirates **attacked** a ship, they had to decide what to do:

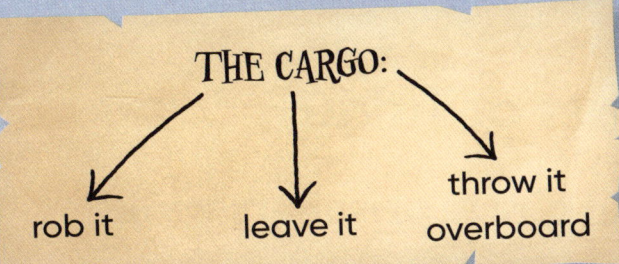

Fact or fake?

Did pirate prisoners walk the plank?

There is **not much evidence** that pirates made prisoners walk off a plank into the sea. Instead, enemies were thrown overboard or dragged behind the ship by a rope.

Life on a pirate ship was not easy. The surroundings were
not very comfortable!

Pirates slept on the floor, or in hammocks.

CAPTAIN TEACH

In 1717, Teach became captain of the *Revenge*. Teach **robbed** many ships with the *Revenge*. He captured some and sank others. But he **always** set the crews **free**.

However, writers at the time didn't mention this. This produced the idea that Teach was **violent** and **dangerous**.

Blackbeard has been remembered this way ever since.

Fact or fake?

Pirate treasure

We think of pirate treasure as gold, silver and jewels. However, pirates usually stole **less exciting** items, such as cloth, rope and sugar. The pirates kept these supplies or sold them to make money.

Lots of people think that pirates **buried** their treasure. However, there is **not much evidence** that they did!

What is your favourite pirate fact so far?

In late 1717, the *Revenge* came across a French ship in the Caribbean Sea. It was called *La Concorde*.

La Concorde was used to transport enslaved people from their home country. The ship was **large**, so Teach was keen to capture it.

The *Revenge* was smaller and *faster*. It could chase *La Concorde* down.

When the *Revenge* got close, it fired its cannons. Iron cannonballs destroyed *La Concorde*'s sails. Now it **could not move**.

The pirates swung from ropes onto *La Concorde*. The ship was **theirs**. They took the ship to a Caribbean island. They left the crew and enslaved people there.

Then the pirates refitted the ship. They made room for the **maximum** number of cannons. They changed the sails to make the ship *faster.*

Teach renamed *La Concorde* the **Queen Anne's Revenge**. The name came from the war he fought in as a young sailor.

Now Teach was a **pirate captain,** with one of the **largest** ships on the sea.

Queen Anne's Revenge

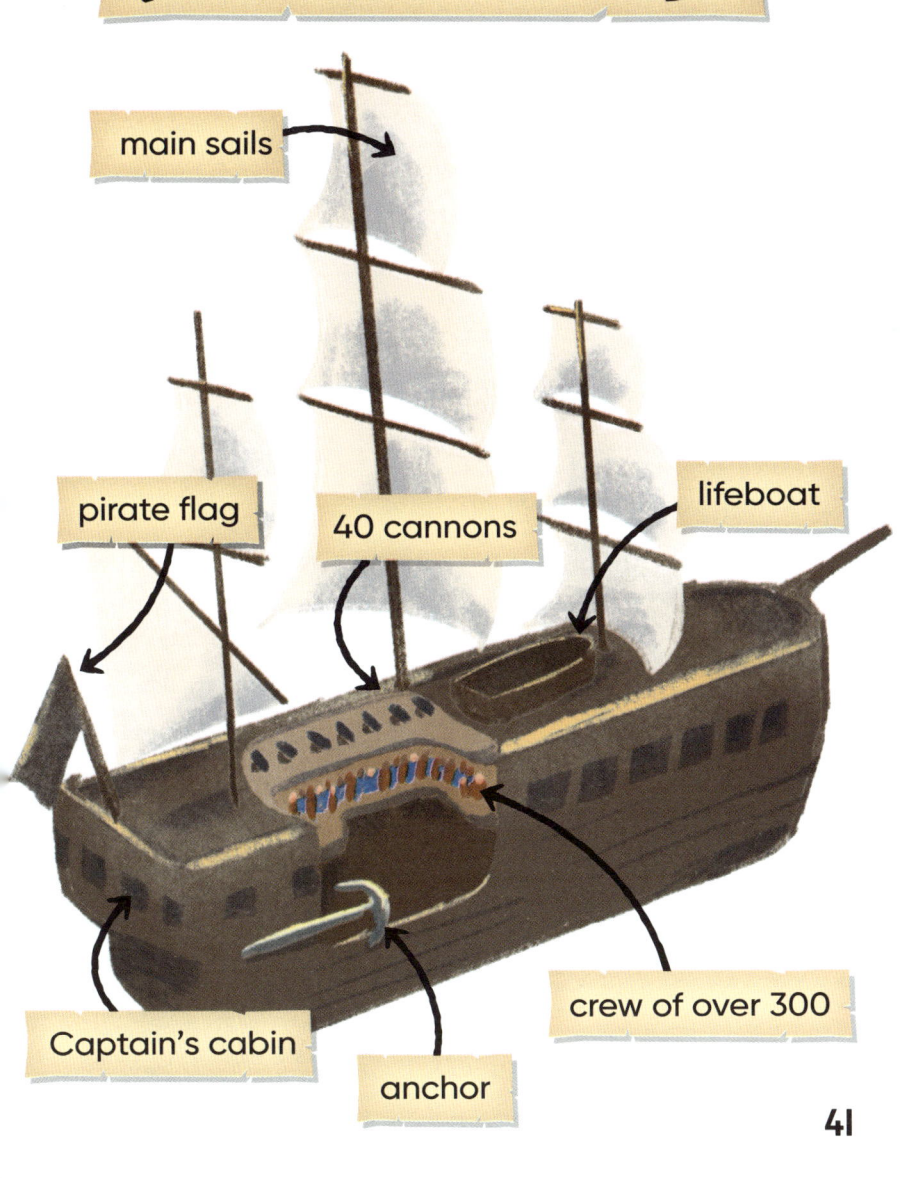

- main sails
- pirate flag
- 40 cannons
- lifeboat
- Captain's cabin
- anchor
- crew of over 300

41

In 1996, the **SHIPWRECK** of the *Queen Anne's Revenge* was found. Objects discovered on the ship included a bell, some cannons and an anchor.

anchor

No one is sure what Blackbeard's **flag** looked like. It may have been this:

or this:

or this:

In December 1717, Teach **captured** a merchant ship. The pirates stole the ship's cargo and made its crew **hostages**.

After being released, the ship's captain, Henry Bostock, described his memory of Teach.

Bostock said Teach had:

"a very black beard which he wore very long".

From then on, Teach became known to the world as **Blackbeard**.

BLACKBEARD: THE LEGEND

Teach was pleased to be known as the **fearsome** captain Blackbeard. If people recognized and **feared** him, they would give him what he wanted.

He worked carefully on his style. He dressed in **black**, braided his beard and attached **BURNING** matches under his hat. This meant smoke blew around his face.

Blackbeard the legend was born!

Blackbeard was soon in charge of **hundreds of pirates**. He had an entire **fleet of ships**. He was now a **major threat** to all ships in the Caribbean Sea and on North America's east coast.

'**Captain**' no longer sounded grand enough to Blackbeard. So, he began calling himself **Commodore** (say: com-uh-daw). Commodores are more important than captains.

In the early 1700s, North America was under the control of Britain. It was known as British America.

Blackbeard was such a **threat** that a local leader in British America sent a letter to Britain's King George I (say: George the First) asking for help.

King George I

51

BLACKBEARD'S END

In June 1718, Blackbeard did something no pirate had tried before. He sailed his fleet into the port of Charles Town. He blocked all ships going in or out. Then he **captured** nine or ten ships. He locked up their crews as **hostages**.

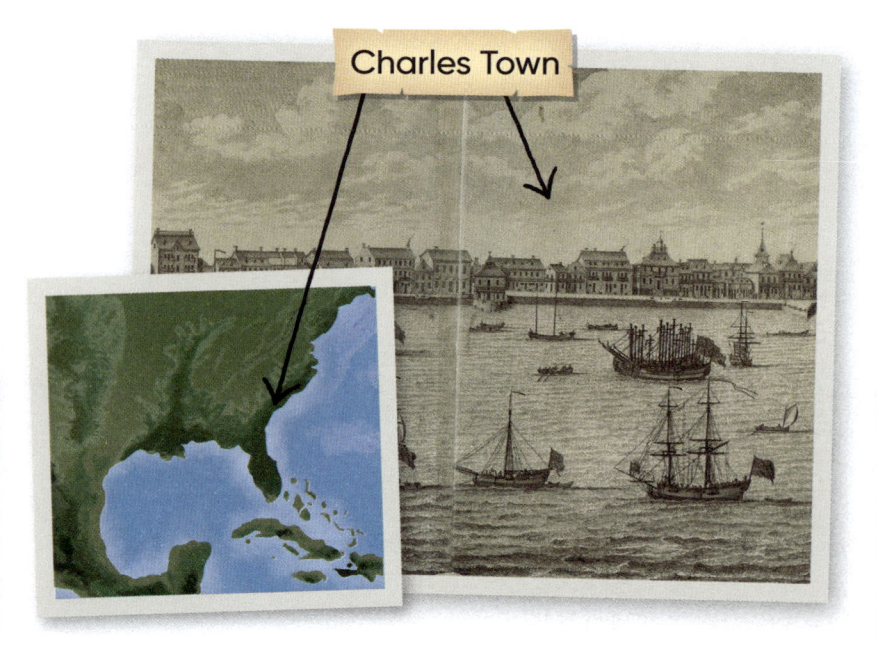

Charles Town

The people of Charles Town were *terrified*. What did Blackbeard want? A chest full of treasure?

No, a chest full of medicine!

Blackbeard said if he didn't get this medicine, he would harm the hostages.

The town gave Blackbeard a chest of medicine. Then Blackbeard **released** the hostages and sailed away.

However, now people wanted Blackbeard to be **stopped**.

After leaving Charles Town, Blackbeard wanted to hide and repair his ships. However, two navy **pirate-hunting** ships were sent to find Blackbeard.

His luck was running out.

In November 1718, the navy ships found Blackbeard's ship. A battle broke out.

The navy soldiers boarded Blackbeard's ship. They fought with pistols and cutlasses.

In the end, the pirates lost.
Blackbeard was killed.

Fact or fake?

Blackbeard's legacy

When Blackbeard died, people thought he had killed lots of people. However, we are now only sure he killed **one person**. This was during his last battle.

In truth, we know little about Blackbeard. Our only information comes from newspapers, letters and one book.

This book was written by Charles Johnson, after Blackbeard died. It describes the lives of famous pirates.

Blackbeard is remembered for a combination of reasons. He looked terrifying and everyone thought he was a **BLOODTHIRSTY KILLER**. However, we now know lots of the information in Charles Johnson's book was **wrong**.

So, what about Blackbeard is **true** and what is **false?** We will never know for sure. However, we do know that the world still sees him as he wanted to be remembered:

the fearsome pirate captain, Blackbeard.

This photo of Blackbeard is from a film.

GLOSSARY

bloodthirsty: eager to hurt or kill

cargo: goods transported by ship or other vehicle

crews: groups of people who run a ship

cutlasses: short, curved swords

enslaved: an enslaved person is captured and forced to work against their will

During Blackbeard's time, capturing people was a business. People were captured mostly from the continent of Africa. Then they were sold to people in America and Britain. This cruel practice was banned in 1838 in Britain and 1865 in North America.

hanged: when a person is killed by hanging them from a rope around their neck

hostages: people who are held prisoner until the people who are holding them get what they want

merchant ships: ships that carry cargo or people

pistols: small guns

privately-owned: belonging to a person or group of people

INDEX

Benjamin Hornigold 24-25

Blackbeard's childhood 20

British Navy 21, 55-56

Charles Town 52-56

King George I 50-51

La Concorde 36-39

pirate life 30-31

pirate myths 12-13, 28-29, 34-35

privateers...21-23

the *Queen Anne's Revenge* 39-42

the *Revenge*................................32, 36-37

LOOK BACK

1. How did Blackbeard become a pirate?

2. Do you think Blackbeard was a hero or a criminal? Explain your answer.

3. How was Blackbeard eventually caught in 1718?

4. Why do you think people are so interested in pirates?

HA! HA!

What is a pirate's favourite lesson?

Arrrrrrt!

READ OUT LOUD

Sea shanties were songs sung by pirates and sailors. Let's see if you can sing one.

The Coast of High Barbary is a famous pirate shanty. It is about a British Navy ship hunting down pirates, just like those that chased Blackbeard. The Coast of Barbary was an area of North Africa.

Warm up your voice and get practising! Read the song aloud first before you try to sing it. Try it one verse at a time.

song

THE COAST OF HIGH BARBARY

There was a gallant English ship
A-sailing on the sea,
Blow high, blow low,
and so say we.
And her Captain he was searching
For a pirate enemy,
Cruising down along the coast
Of the High Barbary.

'O if you're a jolly pirate
Then I'd have you come this way',
Blow high, blow low,
and so say we;
'Bring out your coat of guns boys,
And we'll show this pirates' play.'
Cruising down along the coast
Of the High Barbary.

READ IT AGAIN

1. Try adding some actions to the sea shanty and sing it again. Then try singing it like a pirate, or Blackbeard himself!

2. Look up the other verses of the sea shanty on the internet with an adult. Try singing the shanty again, this time with all the verses.

3. Then try memorizing a verse from the sea shanty. See if you can sing it without needing the book.

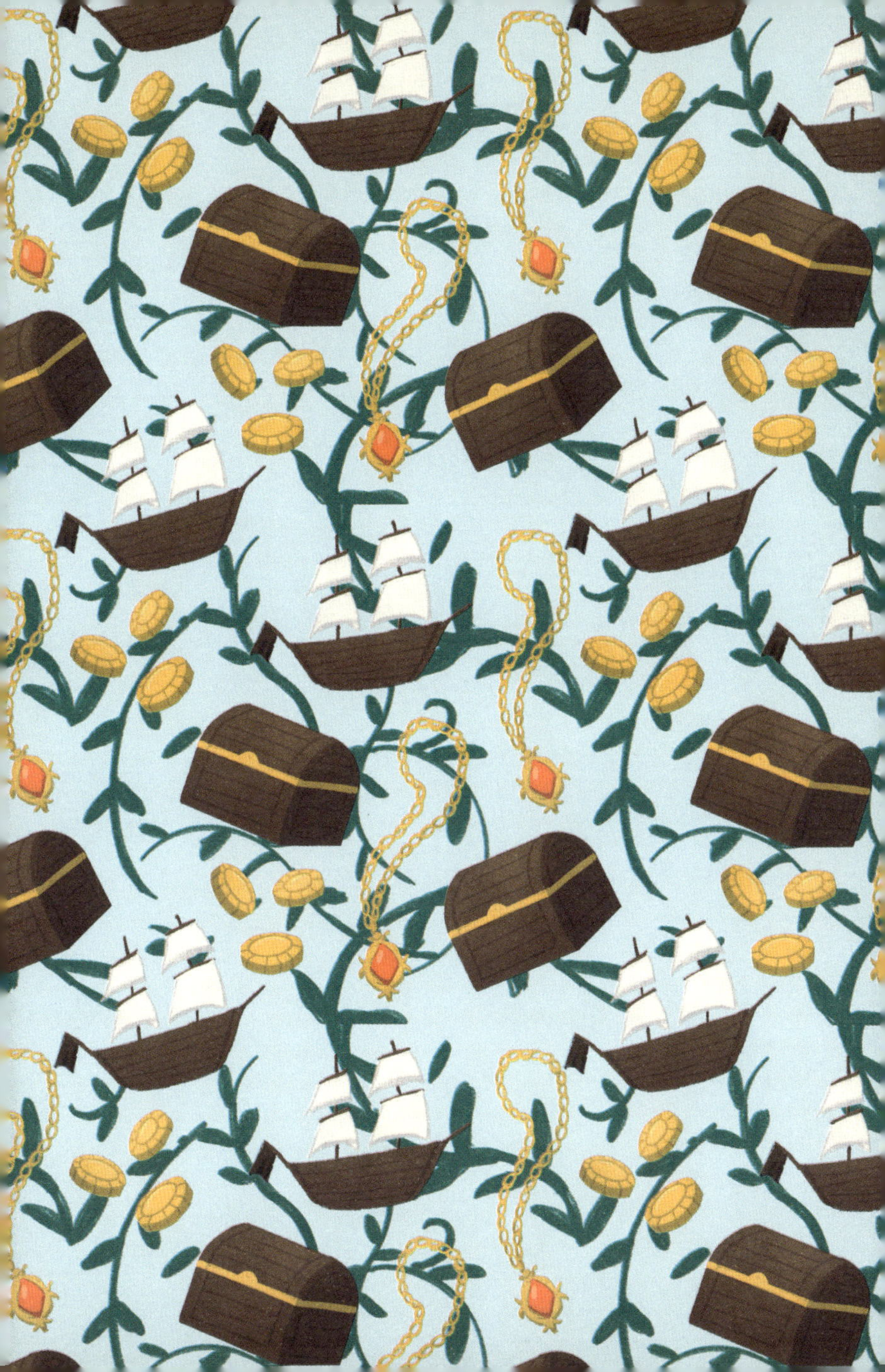

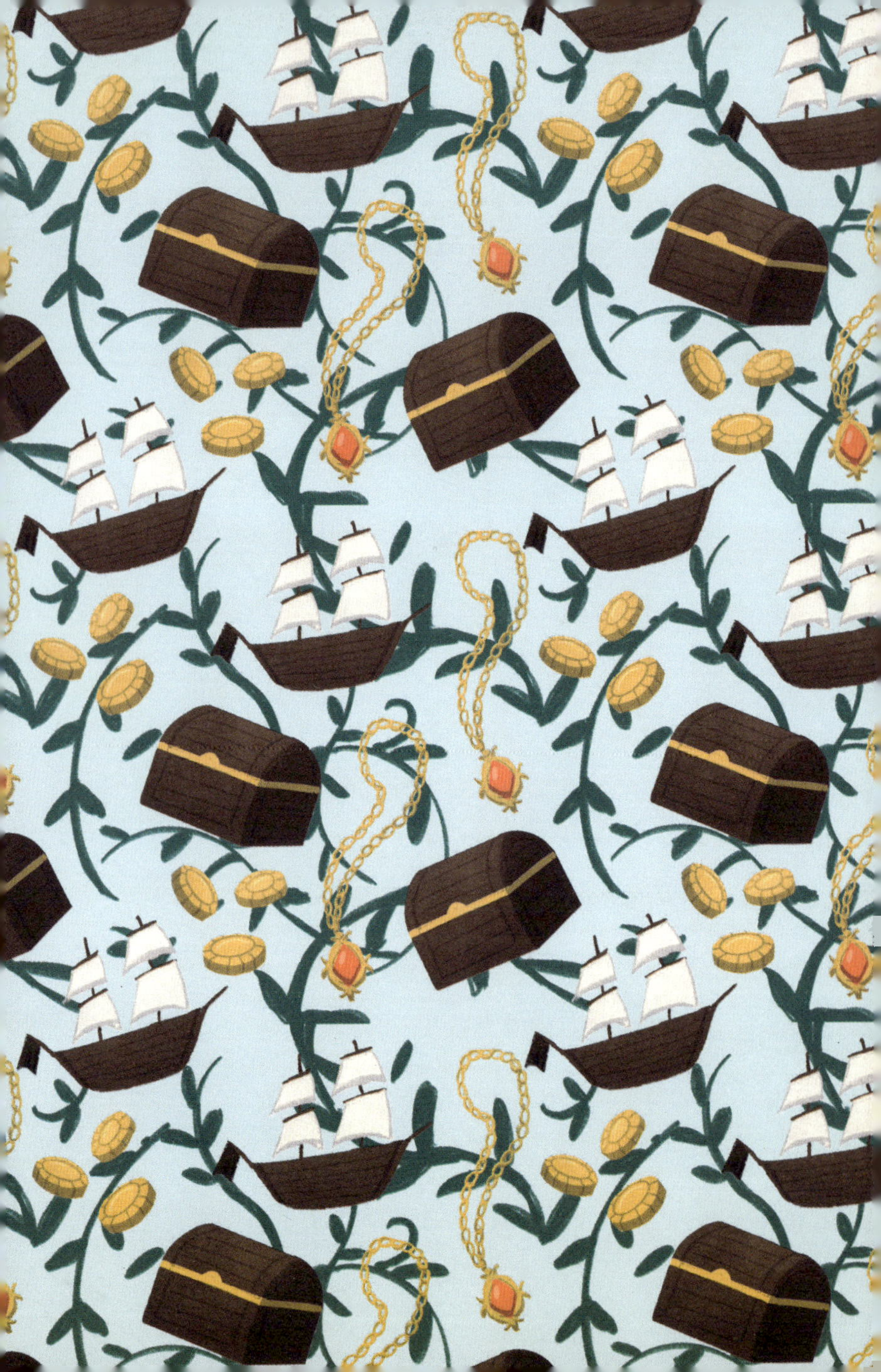